Unlocking Your Sixth Sense:

An Easy Guide to Psychic Development

6/23

Unlocking Your Sixth Sense:

An Easy Guide to Psychic Development

Jacqui Geary

First Edition: May 2017

Copyright © 2017 by Jacqui Geary

Gilmore Publishing

ISBN: 978-0-9990004-0-3

Cover and Book Design by
Dana Bree
www.stonebeardesign.com
Art from Shutterstock

Dedication

To God, Jesus and Archangel Michael for guiding me and always having my back.

To my awesome children Robbie and Katlyn whom I love with all of my heart. The apples did not fall far from the weirdness tree.

To my supportive family, Jill, Dave, Emma, Kyle and Cameron. I love you and yes, you are all weirdos too.

To my passed Loved Ones for watching over me from above. I know I've kept you busy.

To Mommy, for encouraging me from heaven to finish this book. I did it! I love and miss you so very much.

Table of Contents

In Loving Memory of Darlene Gindhart. An inspiring and angelic soul who touched so many lives. Not a day goes by that you are not loved and missed, my beautiful friend. I will cherish our friendship always.

You are in our hearts forever.

"Tears are God's gift to us. Our Holy Water. They heal us as they flow."
- Rita Schiano

Acknowledgements

Special Thanks to:

Dana Bree for her encouragement, support and faith in me as well as her help in putting this book together and for designing an amazing cover.

To Mark Stinziano for his high spirits, unwavering support and belief in all we do. Special thanks for picking up the extra work so I could have time to finish this book.

To Janine Rohm for having one of the kindest hearts I have ever known and for taking time to edit this book.

To all of you who take part in my psychic development class for trusting me to teach you what I know and for making class so fun and entertaining.

I am full of gratitude and love for you all.

"*Psychic development is a necessary skill in leading a successful and happy life. Your intellectual processes and your senses don't give you enough information to distinguish the real from the unreal.*"

-Frederick Lenz

Introduction

For as long as I can remember, beginning at a very young age, I was intrigued with the mysterious and unexplained. I was drawn to all things strange and unusual. I loved to read any mystery book I could find along with books about ghosts, UFO's and Bigfoot. At the age of five, I remember seeing my first spirits. They roamed around at night and I could see their shadows and silhouettes in the dimness of my night-light lit room. My bedroom could never be completely dark. When all of the lights were off, I could see their faces. There seemed to be more spirits around when it was completely dark. I would become so scared I could hardly breathe and my heart felt like it was beating out of my chest. At some point each night, I would eventually run into my parent's room and climb into bed with them. I learned if I slept with the TV and lights on, it helped, as I realized that if the lights were off and all was quiet, I could not only see them but I could hear them as well. Although I may have been scared of the existence of spirits during my childhood years, the thought of another realm became increasingly appealing to me. I participated in my first ghost hunt during my senior year of high school. My ghost-hunting journey has been an amazing one, but it's a whole other story for a whole other book.

During my middle school years I began to realize I didn't "feel" good around certain people for no apparent reason. In some of those instances I wouldn't know anything about the person and in those moments, I had the intense feeling to keep it that way. I had the feeling it was not someone I should get too close to. Although there were times when I had a creepy feeling around particular people, there were other times when I would see a person and know we would become good friends. In high school I had many experiences of déjà vu (Déjà vu is the feeling "this already happened"). I remember I was talking to a friend while getting books out of my locker. All of a sudden I just stopped talking. My friend asked me what was wrong and I told her I was sure we already had this same exact conversation. It felt like I had previously lived that moment. Of course at the time I did not know it was déjà vu.

As I learned more about the paranormal, I became aware of the different types of abilities and phenomenons.

When I was a child, a family friend gave us a stack of board games her children no longer used. In that pile of games was the Amazing Kreskin's ESP Board Game, which soon became one of my favorites, along with CLUE, of course! I was fascinated by the mystery pendulum, the symbol cards and color cards because I always seemed to "guess" right. I would see the color in my head or just seem to know the right answer. Although I did not realize it, I was working on developing my psychic abilities while playing the game. Kreskin's ESP Board Game became an outlet for me explore my interest in the mysteries of the unknown. I had the opportunity of meeting the Amazing Kreskin last year. It was a humbling experience to meet the person who invented the game that was destined to become a part of my life. That game was meant to be in the pile of games which were dropped off. *"Everything happens for a reason"* my mom used to say and, as she did every day of her life, I now live by this quote, too. We may not know in the moment why something happens, we only need to have faith and trust that everything will turn out just as it should.

At birthday parties I jumped at participating in playing the scary and creepy sleepover games like "Stiff as a board, Light as a feather". Without question I was one of the first to join in on sharing ghost stories and urban legends. A few years ago I ran into a childhood friend at one of my center's annual paranormal events. She was not surprised my livelihood was in the metaphysical and paranormal fields. She reminded me of all the times we dabbled in the paranormal as kids. It was a great affirmation I am living my life's purpose.

Having the ability to do "weird" things was not something I shared with everyone when I was a child. At that time, the paranormal was not a subject often talked about. The person I did talk to was my mother. When I was a little girl and told her I saw ghosts she never made me feel weird. She would ask me *"What did they look like?"* When I would tell her I did not feel comfortable around someone, she would say, *"Well there must be a reason you are feeling that way. Listen to your feelings."* When I would tell her I had dreams that would come true a few days later, she told me she sometimes had those same types of dreams, too. I did not feel "weird" around my mother. In later years we would watch the psychic shows on TV together. She especially looked forward to watching Sylvia Browne when she would appear on The Montel Williams Show. My mom passed on to Heaven almost ten years ago, but she is with me every day as I move forward on this spiritual path. I am grateful to her for encouraging me to feel comfortable with being different and I am happy to pay it forward by encouraging and teaching others how to do the same.

Thankfully, as time went on, my interest in the metaphysical and paranormal fields widened. This, in turn, has paved the way for more available avenues for those of us who choose to raise our awareness and embrace our psychic gifts. I kept my psychic and mediumship abilities tucked away from others for a long time. A life changing experience altered that for me and led the way to my spiritual journey to help others. Many of my family members have psychic abilities and we are proud to talk about them with each other. My sister Jill Motcheck shares a memory: "As I laid in bed as a young child, I saw my dad's father walk into my parent's bedroom. I never met my grandfather before he passed on. I didn't know it was him until years later when I saw his picture. To this day I see spirit shadows and receive intuitive guidance from my angels, guides and loved ones."

In this book, I share the tips and techniques I use to tune into and strengthen my own psychic abilities. Everyone is naturally intuitive and we all have a degree of psychic ability in some way or another. No matter what your age, you can develop your psychic gifts. We are all unique. We are spiritual energies in a physical vehicle, making our human side our toughest challenge in psychic development. You will learn how to overcome that challenge. Feel free to use whichever skills or techniques in this book work best for you. It may be all of them; it may be just a few. As long as you stay consistent and make a commitment to yourself to develop your psychic abilities, you will. Enjoy the Journey! :-)

"The things that make me different are the things that make me ME."
− (Piglet), A.A. Milne, Winnie-the-Pooh

I believe in the value of inspirational quotes so I have included a selection of my favorites through-out this book.

"One powerful quote could change your life."
- Jacqui Geary

* * ** * * * * * * * * * ** * * ** * * * * * * * * * * * ** * *

"The wisdom of the wise, and the experience of ages, may be preserved by quotation."
- Isaac D'Israeli

* * ** * * * * * * * ** * * ** * * * * * * * * * * * ** * *

"Every man is a quotation from all his ancestors."
- Ralph Waldo Emerson

* * ** * * * * * * * ** * * ** * * * * * * * * * * * ** * *

"An apt quotation is like a lamp which flings its light over the whole sentence."
- Letitia Elizabeth Landon

How Psychic Development Changed My Life

"I have been going to psychic development for about five years and it centers me and allows me to be in the most unjudgmental places I have ever been, and I crave that in my life and I deserve it. It helps me cope with every area of my life."

- Charles Bodnar

✳ ✳✳ ✳ ✳ ✳ ✳ ✳ ✳ ✳ ✳ ✳✳ ✳ ✳ ✳ ✳ ✳ ✳ ✳ ✳ ✳ ✳ ✳ ✳ ✳ ✳ ✳ ✳✳ ✳ ✳

"One of the first things I learned from Jacqui in her psychic development classes was being able to just relax and not overthink. I used to struggle to find an answer to the lesson presented. I tried so hard to come up with a solution and would fail each time. And each time she would tell me to not overthink, trust the first response that comes. I finally got it

and stopped worrying about right or wrong answers. From then on I really started to grow.

Jacqui is one of those rare people who does not jealously guard her secrets but instead shares what she knows. Her joy is in teaching and seeing us all develop in ways we did not think possible."
- Dana Bree

* * ** * * * * * * * * * * ** * * * * * * * * * * * * * * * ** * *

"Since I started attending Jacqui's classes I have learned so many things-about myself and how I view the world. The most profound is the amazing feeling of peace that I have in my life now every day. I can honestly say that her classes have changed my life-for the better!"
- Darlene Gindhart

* * ** * * * * * * * * ** * * * * * * ** * * ** * * * * * ** * *

"When I mention to my friends that I take psychic development, most ask me if I am learning to read minds. I simply smile a crooked smile and tell them no. Psychic development with Jacqui Geary has

opened a closed mind to so many things. It has taught me to better understand where others are coming from as well as understanding myself. I have learned to understand and interpret that "nagging feeling" or "voice in my ear" into actual useable information for others. Through her meditations and teachings, I have learned to shed many of the negative Aries traits and enhance the good ones. I have seen miracles performed by this beautiful yet humble woman. She has brought me closer to God, myself and others. She has taught me the value of staying on your path. I only wish you reading this can have your life touched as she has mine. Oh and yes.... she has taught me to read your mind.

- Mark Stinziano

"*Your sixth sense sees the unseen, hears the unspoken, and knows the untold.*"
- Phil Good

"*We each have a sixth sense that is attuned to the oneness dimension in life, providing a means for us to guide our lives in accord with our ideas.*"
- Henry Ree

1

The Sixth Sense

What is the "Sixth Sense"? Do you ever feel like you just "know" things? Do you sometimes "feel" things about certain situations or people? The sixth sense is the sense beyond the five basic physical senses of sight, touch, taste, smell and hearing. The physical senses tune into what physically exists around us while our sixth sense tunes into subtler, non-physical sensations, otherwise known as our intuition. This extraordinary sense we all have, otherwise known as ESP (extra sensory perception) or as some refer to it, our "*spidey sense*", enables our ability to perceive the unseen. By using our sixth sense, along with tuning into our other five senses, we can receive intuitive and psychic information. We can develop our sixth sense by increasing our spiritual level, particularly through psychic development.

When you just "know" there's something you can't put your finger on. Whether it's about someone you feel isn't trustworthy or when you turn left (and end up lost) even though you "knew" you should have turned right—that is your intuition guiding you. We all have free will, so ultimately the choice is ours whether to trust our intuition or not. Practicing psychic development will help you learn the difference between your inner voice and your free will.

We are all naturally intuitive. Our intuition taps into our subconscious for guidance. It is the guidance we receive without any conscious thought. We receive intuitive information every day. The key to tapping in to our sixth sense is learning how to open our awareness, thus enabling us to tune in to our intuition so we can receive our messages. When we use our intuition we are listening to our "gut feeling". It's that sense that comes to you in a flash and can encompass you. When you are using your intuition you have a knowing of things without reason and are able to have insight and see within. Intuition and psychic abilities provide needed guidance for the self and others. The more often you listen to your intuition, the stronger it will grow.

"If prayer is you talking to God, then Intuition is God talking to you."
- Dr. Wayne Dyer

✳ ✳ ✳✳ ✳ ✳ ✳ ✳ ✳ ✳ ✳ ✳ ✳✳ ✳ ✳ ✳ ✳ ✳ ✳ ✳ ✳ ✳ ✳ ✳ ✳ ✳ ✳ ✳✳ ✳ ✳

"Intuition is the supra-logic that cuts out all the routine processes of thought and leaps straight from the problem to the answer."
-Robert Graves

✳ ✳ ✳✳ ✳ ✳ ✳ ✳ ✳ ✳ ✳ ✳✳ ✳ ✳ ✳ ✳ ✳ ✳ ✳ ✳ ✳ ✳ ✳ ✳ ✳ ✳ ✳ ✳✳ ✳ ✳

"Intuition literally means learning from within.

Most of us were not taught how to use this sense, but all of us know well that "gut" feeling. Learn to trust your inner feeling and it will become stronger. Avoid going against your better judgment or getting talked into things that just don't feel right."
- Doe Zantamata

Most people are not even aware of their sixth sense. It has been proven by researchers and scientists that humans have the same ability as animals to sense magnetic fields.

Have you ever noticed an animal acting anxious right before a storm is coming? This is because they are feeling the changes in the electromagnetic field. Many animals including, birds, dolphins and spiders use this ability particularly during migration. Cats and dogs are known to exhibit their sixth sense. Have you noticed a cat or dog staring at an empty corner of a room? He/she may be observing a spirit. Does your family pet snuggle up to you when you are sick?

Sensing you are unwell, your pet is comforting you. Animals have uncanny extrasensory abilities.

A "Psychic" has a highly developed sixth sense. Some are born with it; others are able to develop it in time. We are all born with a certain degree of psychic ability. Some people are open to developing their sixth sense, others are not. The more open you are the higher you will develop. It is important to remember that our psychic information is from spirit and we are just the messenger. These messages are meant to guide us on our path. Your connection to spirit and understanding of these messages will strengthen through psychic development. As we grow spiritually and increase our personal growth, the stronger our abilities become.

Mindfulness will help you become in tune with your five physical senses, in turn making these senses more acute and enhancing your psychic abilities. Close your eyes and listen to the sounds around you—the ticking clock, passing cars, people talking nearby, the leaves rustling in the wind—whatever sounds are around you. Do you smell any scents? Flowers? Candles? Clean, fresh air? What do you feel? Cold? Warm? Peaceful? Now open your eyes. What do you see? A blue sky? Cars driving by? People walking around? Now note how blue the sky is, the smile on someone's face, the colors of the flowers in the vase on the table. This is mindfulness. Awareness of the five physical senses helps to clearly open the sixth sense.

When we fully understand our sixth sense we are able to tap into our intuition, as well as open up our psychic abilities. These abilities, clairvoyance, clairsentience, claircognizance and clairaudience, to name a few, help us perceive beyond our normal being including obtaining information on the past, present and future.

"Our bodies have five senses: Touch, smell, taste, sight, hearing. But not to be overlooked are the

senses of our souls: intuition, peace, foresight, trust, and empathy. The differences between people lie in their use of the senses; most people don't know anything about the inner senses while a few people rely on them just as they rely on their physical senses, and in fact probably even more."
- C. JoyBell C.

* * ** * * * * * * * * * * ** * * * * * * ** * * * * * * * * ** * *

"The intuitive mind is a sacred gift and the rational mind is a faithful servant."
- Albert Einstein

* * ** * * * * * * * * * ** * * * * * * * * * * * * * * * ** * *

"Listen to your intuition. It will tell you everything you need to know."
- Anthony J. D'Angelo

* * ** * * * * * * ** * ** * * * * * * * * * * * * * * * ** * *

"People only see what they are prepared to see."
- Ralph Waldo Emerson

2

The Third Eye and The Chakras

The Third Eye is the Sixth Chakra (otherwise known as The Brow) and is the gateway to our psychic abilities and higher consciousness. The Third Eye is connected to the Pineal Gland. This tiny gland controls the endocrine system, including sleeping patterns. Due to the control the pineal gland has over our endocrine system, it influences our energy channels. Awakening the Third Eye helps us achieve deeper insight and enlightenment. The Third Eye can see beyond the physical, thus the belief it is the connection between the physical and spiritual worlds.

During the awakening process you may feel pressure in your head or experience headaches. This is a common occurrence throughout psychic development and can also result when the Third Eye is over stimulated.

"It's not what you look at that matters, it's what you see."

- Henry Davis Thoreau

TIP: The following are a few types of essential oils that are beneficial for opening and balancing the Third Eye Chakra.

Jasmine - Enhances intuition, healing and our connectedness to the Universe

Palo Santo - Increases spiritual awareness, used for cleansing energy and in meditation

Clary Sage - Cleanses energy field, removal and

protection of negative energy

Frankincense - Grounding, calming, increases spiritual awareness

Rose - Balances, relaxes, raises vibration

Sandalwood - Grounding, calming, installs inner peace

Chamomile - Calming, keeps ego balanced

As an aromatic purpose essential oils can be diffused in various types of diffusers or wax warmers (use essential oil in place of wax cube). There are a variety of essential oils that can be beneficial for opening and balancing the Third Eye. If you are familiar with essential oils you may already be using one of the above listed types. You may have your own personal blend of oil you resonate with and choose to work specifically. Whichever oil you feel compelled to use is the one for you.

* * ** * ** * *

Third Eye Chakra Affirmation: "I SEE"

* * ** * ** * *

Chakras are the energy centers of the physical body. Each of these energy centers correlate to particular glands, organs and functions in the body, as well as our consciousness. The chakras are associated with our physical, mental and emotional states. The Sanskrit word Chakra means "wheel" or circle describing its function of spinning energy. There are seven major chakras. When balanced, these energy centers are open and spinning at the same rate. Many times, our chakras are out of balance and blocked or closed, due to our life experiences and our reactions to those experiences. Chakra balancing can be achieved through energy work, meditation, visualization, breath work and other alternative ways of restoring the natural flow of energy.

The seven major chakras are located along the spine. They start at the base of the spine and move up to the top of the head. Each chakra is represented by a color.

Seven Major Chakras:

First Chakra - Root – red, foundation, survival, grounding, located at base of spine

Second Chakra - Sacral – orange, emotions, desires/pleasure, and intimacy, located below the navel

Third Chakra - Solar Plexus – yellow, the self (self-worth, self-esteem)/feelings, personal power, located above the navel

Fourth Chakra - Heart – green, love, inner peace, well being, located at the center of the chest

Fifth Chakra - Throat – blue, communication, self-expression, creativity, located in the throat

Sixth Chakra - Third Eye (Brow) – indigo, intuition, psychic senses, clarity, located in the center of the forehead between your eyebrows

Seventh Chakra - Crown – violet, spirituality, enlightenment, understanding, located at the top of the head

Balancing your chakras will enhance your psychic abilities by increasing the flow of information you receive.

"Intuition is a spiritual faculty and does not explain, but simply points the way."

- Florence Scovel Shinn

* * ** * * * * * * * * ** * * * * * * * * * * * * * * ** * *

"Intuition goes before you, showing you the way. Emotion falls behind, to let you know when you go astray. Listen to your inner voice. It is the calling of your spiritual GPS system seeking to keep you on track towards your true destiny."

- Anthon St. Maarten

3

Opening Your Intuitive Awareness

Opening your awareness heightens your sixth sense. So how do we open our awareness so that we just have the knowing that the information we are receiving is our intuition and not our thoughts? Through our belief, trust, intent, practice and expectations!

But first we **must** meditate.

Meditation, Meditation, Meditation

We are spiritual energies in a physical vehicle. We

need to consciously be aware to ground and center ourselves as often as possible. Meditation is the best way to achieve this. I begin each psychic development class I teach with a meditation. It is a key step to helping you open your awareness. Meditation helps us to relax, quiet our mind, release the stress of our day and open up our energy. It will be helpful whether you have only ten minutes to meditate or an hour. You must work to raise your personal vibration, as spirit energy is a higher vibration. Maintaining a higher vibration is needed to consistently tune in to these spiritual energies. Some people have difficulty quieting their mind when meditating. If you have busy thoughts, just before meditating, close your eyes and visualize putting all of those thoughts into a bin or basket. When learning to meditate, it may take a few times or many times to quiet the mind, but eventually it will come about after practice. Do not give up! I have had students who had an extremely hard time quieting their mind. Sometimes it takes weeks of practice and conditioning the mind to relax. Be patient. Each time you meditate you are working at raising your awareness even if you do not see the immediate results. A helpful tip is to listen to relaxing, healing music while falling asleep. The sound therapy of the music works subliminally to relax your mind and can aid in the process of meditating. Do not worry about whether you will be able to meditate or not...just be in the moment.

Guided and unguided meditations can be found in books, CDs and online. There are various types of free meditations available. If you choose you may want to script and record your own meditation. Record your voice reciting the meditation with soothing background music, and then listen back to what you have recorded as a guided meditation. I have included a guided meditation on the next page that I use in my psychic development class.

Tip: Sit or lay in a relaxed and comfortable position while meditating. It is believed facing palms up during meditation helps open the flow of energy. Taking off your shoes aids in spiritual connectedness and grounding.

"*Meditation brings wisdom; lack of meditation leaves ignorance. Know well what leads you forward and what holds you back, and choose the path that leads to wisdom.*"

- Buddha

Awakening Your Intuitive Abilities Guided Meditation

Play calm, relaxing music.

Lie down or sit in a comfortable position.

Close your eyes.

Take three long, deep breaths.

(pause)

Now imagine a beautiful white light surrounding you.

Allow the light to fill up your entire body.

See the light begin to swirl,

Up through your feet,

Through your body,

Through your throat,

Up to the center of your forehead,

And now between your eyes.

This is your third eye,

Your place of psychic perception.

See the light turn a deep blue,

Circling and opening your awareness.

See the light expand.

Feel the energy as your third eye begins to open.

See it open with a vibrant burst of light.

Feel the energy.

Feel its power.

(pause)

Your intuitive awareness is now opening,

Increasing and expanding,

Now see the light move up to just above the top of your head,

See it swirling around,

Turning into a vibrant purple light,

Circling above the top of your head,

Opening your crown chakra,

See the light becoming brighter,

Now, using your inner eye, look up and out through the top of your head,

You see a deep blue circle of light glowing above,

Streaming in through your head in a beautiful shimmering light,

Feel the light surround your head and mind,

Feel your intuitive powers awaken,

See your third eye as it begins to glow,

See the light becoming brighter and brighter,

Feel it expanding.

Focus on the deep blue color radiating from your third eye.

(pause)

Now see the light as it moves down to your throat,

Slowly moving to your heart area,

Moving down to your stomach,

Down to just below the navel area,

Moving down through your lower spine,

Through your legs,

And then down into your feet.

See the light move through your feet,

Going deep into the earth,

Attaching to the center of the earth.

Now feel the new revitalizing energy entering your body as the light moves back up,

The earth's energy,

Circling and moving up through the bottom of your feet,

Up through your legs,

Through your lower spine,

Through your navel,

Through your stomach,

Up through your heart,

Through your throat,

Up to your third eye,

Then moving to just above the top of your head,

Creating energy and power above the top of your head.

Opening your head as a gateway to the universe.

See the bright light evenly flowing up and out of your head

Up into the sky,

Connecting you to All That Is,

Opening your intuition,

Opening your awareness.

Take three deep breaths,

Slowly open your eyes.

Believe and Trust

If you do not believe, you will not receive. Self-doubt and negative thoughts can impede psychic ability. Your subconscious mind must believe you can receive to enable use of your psychic gifts. Our blockages are held in our subconscious mind. If you do not trust and believe that you can develop your abilities, you will block yourself from doing so. Fear will crush your confidence. Have the trust and belief that you can and will develop your psychic abilities. Trust your intuition and sense of knowing. Trust what you are receiving to be accurate and that it is guiding you in the right direction, to the best outcome. You may not be comfortable when first starting to use your abilities. That is ok. When you are uncomfortable that means you are growing. You will experience a lot of growth during psychic development!

"The mind is everything.
What you think you become."
– Buddha

"Everything is energy and that's all there is to it.
Match the frequency of the reality you want and you
cannot help but get that reality. It can be no other
way. This is not philosophy. This is physics."
- Albert Einstein

* * ** * * * * * * * * * ** * * * * * * * * * * * * * * * ** * *

"It's not who you are that holds you back, it's who
you think you're not."
- Author Unknown

Intention

The purity of your intention is key to highly developing your psychic abilities. Maintain good intention on why and how you will use your abilities. The intent should never be for self-gain, but for guiding the self and others. Regardless of what we outwardly say, the Universe always knows the true intent of our subconscious.

Always use your abilities with positive intention, knowledge, integrity and respect. Intent also incorporates focus. Stay focused on what you are working on achieving. It is easy to become distracted, especially if you are frustrated with your progress or are struggling to develop a particular ability. When you feel this way, stop, take three deep breaths, and start again. Keep your intent positive and stay focused.

Tip: Be grateful and thankful for the information you receive. Gratitude brings in more of that which you are already grateful.

"Be thankful for what you have; you'll end up having more. If you concentrate on what you don't have, you will never, ever have enough."
- Oprah Winfrey

* * ** * * * * * * * * * ** * * * * * * * * * * * * * * ** * *

"Such a simple concept, yet so true: that which we manifest is before us; we are the creators of our own destiny. Be it through intention or ignorance, our successes and our failures has been brought on by none other than ourselves."
- Garth Stein

* * ** * * * * * * * * * ** * * * * * * * * * * * * * * ** * *

"Intention is one of the most powerful forces there is. What you mean when you do a thing always determines the outcome. The law creates the world."
- Brenna Yovanoff

* * ** * * * * * * * * * ** * * * * * * * * * * * * * * ** * *

"Successful people maintain a positive focus in life

no matter what is going on around them. They stay focused on their past successes rather than their past failures, and on the next action steps they need to take to get them closer to the fulfillment of their goals rather than all the other distractions that life presents to them."

- Jack Canfield

Practice

Developing your psychic abilities is the same as developing any other type of ability. It requires practice—practice—and more practice. You must commit to daily practice to consistently open and strengthen your abilities. The more often you work on your psychic development skills the better you will learn how to understand and fine tune your intuitive and psychic abilities. It is much like physical therapy. To rebuild and strengthen an injured part of the physical body we must commit to regularly exercising that area. At first the area may be weak and we may not be able to use it at full capacity. As we progress with the physical therapy the area becomes healthier and stronger. It works the same way with the sixth sense. The more you exercise your sixth sense, the stronger and more accurate it becomes.

"For the things we have to learn before we can do them, we learn by doing them."
- Aristotle

"We are what we repeatedly do. Excellence therefore is not an act but a habit."
- Aristotle

"Practice isn't the thing you do once you're good. It's the thing you do that makes you good."
- Malcolm Gladwell

Expectations

One of the major blocks to developing psychic abilities is the expectations one puts on themself to receive information. No Pressure. Expect to receive. Whether you receive one word and one image, or fifty words and twenty images it doesn't matter. You will receive whatever you are meant to receive. Do not compare your abilities to the abilities of others. Each one of us has our own uniqueness in regards to our psychic abilities. Be humble and grateful for whatever abilities you are gifted. Do not worry how quickly or how slowly you progress. Take your time. Just BE. Enjoy the journey. You will block your energy from receiving if you are not open to whatever is meant to come through for you... no matter how much or how little or how long it takes. Be patient. Your relaxed energy will greatly help your progress in psychic development.

"Act without expectation."
- Lao Tzu

* * ** * * * * * * * * * ** * * * * * * * * * * * * * * * ** * *

"Expectation feeds frustration as it's simply an elusive form of control by attempting to grip the reins that aren't ours to hold. Breathe. Release. Let go. Allow your life to naturally, quietly unfold."
- Victoria Erickson

* * ** * * * * * * * * * ** * * * * * * * * * * * * * * * ** * *

"In my life nothing goes wrong. When things seem to not meet my expectations, I let go of how I think things should be. It's a matter of not having any attachment to any fixed outcome."
- Deepak Chopra

* * ** * * * * * * * * * ** * * * * * * * * * * * * * * * ** * *

"A flower does not think of competing to the flower next to it. It just blooms." - Author Unknown

Journaling

Keeping a psychic journal is a helpful tool for understanding and interpreting psychic information, as well as monitoring your progress. I recommend writing down any information you receive randomly throughout the day or while meditating, practicing psychic development and, sleeping/dreaming. This information can be a spur of the moment thought, vision, feeling, something unexplained that you hear or smell, symbols, synchronistic events and so on. Do not dismiss or discount anything, even if it does not make sense to you in that moment...just write it down. After a few days or weeks you may notice a pattern or theme in what you have written down which will help to interpret it. Journaling will also help you become aware of what certain symbols mean for you when receiving psychic information. You can keep a journal for both psychic development exercises and any random information that may come to you throughout the day or you can choose to keep two separate journals. I carry a small pocket sized notebook with me so I can write down information I receive when I'm out and about and often log it on my cell phone using the notes and voice memos apps.

"Don't trust your memory. When you listen to something valuable, write it down. When you come across something important, write it down."
- Jim Rohn

* * ** * * * * * * * * * ** * * * * * * * * * * * * * * ** * *

"Just write every day of your life. Then see what happens."
- Ray Bradbury

4

Overcoming Those Stubborn Blocks

At times you may experience blocks that cause you to feel like you are not moving forward in your psychic development. Maybe you are frustrated that you are not at the level you want to be. Possibly you are having a difficult time developing a particular ability you have been working on. Perhaps the information you are receiving is not as accurate as you would like it to be.

The following are just a few of the most common blocks we all experience and a little guidance that may help you to overcome them.

Overthinking

Overthinking is often the most common block to overcome. Our human side thinks way too much. You do not want to let your thoughts crowd out your intuitive messages. This often occurs if you are naturally an over thinker or have, what I like to call, a "busy" head. Thoughts are often nagging and persistent and they cause you to have a "debate" with yourself inside your head. This is the time the "what ifs" come in. "But what if this happens?" "But what if that happens?" Over and over in your head. You analyze, pull it apart, and try to figure out every angle. Those are your thoughts. Intuitive ideas and information pop into your head with no conscious thought. Sometimes these ideas are in and out in a flash. Often, information is dismissed or second guessed because you may not be sure of whether it is your intuition or not. Sometimes it is dismissed unknowingly because subconsciously it is not the information you want to hear.

Use this simple exercise to help you become more aware of your overthinking:

1. Find a basic object or color to focus on—a red napkin, a purple stone, a green piece of fabric.

2. Make sure you place it on a plain table or in an area where you will not be easily distracted.

3. Close your eyes, take three deep breaths, open your eyes and gaze at the object.

4. How long did you look at the object before your mind became overwhelmed with random thoughts that have nothing to do with the object? 10 seconds? 30 seconds?

5. Write it down.

In the beginning you may start overthinking in the first five seconds. Let's take the purple stone for example. The thoughts of a busy head would be: *"Look at all the cracks. I wonder if those cracks came from it being dropped? The shape of the stone looks like the state of Florida. Maybe I will go to Florida for my next vacation. I bet there are some great seafood places in Florida. What should I make for Dinner?"*

Each time you do this exercise keep track of the length of time it takes before you begin overthinking. You will notice the length of time increases as your mind becomes conditioned to being quieted.

Sometimes when you are trying not to overthink you will be consumed with thinking about overthinking, which can understandably become even more frustrating for you. Meditation is the best technique for overthinking as it helps with quieting the mind and assisting in the awareness of those unnecessary thoughts. If you find you have a hard time meditating due to random thoughts filling your head, just keep practicing. Give yourself time to reprogram your overthinking mind. You may not think you are progressing but each time you meditate you are conditioning your mind to relax. It may take a good deal of practice but eventually it will happen. Remember—no pressure.

"The more I think about it, the more I realize that overthinking isn't the real problem. The real problem is that we don't trust."
- LJ Vanier

✻ ✻✻ ✻ ✻ ✻ ✻ ✻ ✻ ✻ ✻ ✻ ✻✻ ✻ ✻ ✻ ✻ ✻ ✻ ✻ ✻ ✻ ✻ ✻ ✻ ✻ ✻✻ ✻ ✻
"Too much thinking leads to paralysis by analysis."
- Robert Herjavec

✻ ✻ ✻✻ ✻ ✻ ✻ ✻ ✻ ✻ ✻ ✻ ✻✻ ✻ ✻ ✻ ✻ ✻ ✻ ✻ ✻ ✻ ✻ ✻ ✻ ✻ ✻✻ ✻ ✻
"The more you rationalize, the more you move farther away from your authentic self."
- Shannon L. Alder

Ego

The Ego can become a difficult issue to keep in check throughout the development process. As a teacher I have seen the ego affect a student's abilities time and time again. It is important to be grateful for whatever you receive and to not be annoyed if the information cannot be validated at that moment. For instance, suppose you are receiving a message in regards to a friend. You receive an image of your friend standing in a green kitchen and you presume it is their kitchen. They tell you their kitchen is yellow. Do not get discouraged or frustrated that the information you received may not be accurate. Sometimes psychic information can be misinterpreted or the information may not be accurate for that particular moment. It could have been the past or a future image of what is to come. For example, it may be possible the kitchen was green before being painted yellow or perhaps they will be moving to a new house and that is the color of the kitchen. You will not receive validation every time you are given a psychic message and that is okay. Do not get so caught up in the validation that it becomes all consuming. If you are afraid of being wrong in regards to the information you receive, that is your ego at work. If you get caught up in the confirmation of your messages, you may have a tendency to "reach". Examples of reaching would be "Did you have a green kitchen when you were little?" "Do you have a friend, of a friend, of a friend who has a green kitchen?" That is the ego needing validation. Meditate for guidance to help with this issue. Fear and ego will block you from receiving psychic messages accurately.

There may also be a time when you doubt a message or do not like an answer you receive for yourself on a particular subject. This often indicates you are still in a place of personal growth within that area of your life. The first step to overcoming this issue is to acknowledge it, next is to accept it and then you will be able to move forward in that area of your life. Enlightenment is achieved through the shift from the mind and ego to awareness.

"If you want to reach a state of bliss, then go

beyond your ego and the internal dialogue. Make a decision to relinquish the need to control, the need to be approved, and the need to judge. Those are the three things the ego is doing all the time. It's very important to be aware of them every time they come up."
- Deepak Chopra

* * ** * * * * * * * * ** * * * * * * ** * * * * * * ** * *

"You can either be a host to God, or a hostage to your ego. It's your call."
- Wayne Dyer

* * ** * * * * * * ** ** * * * * * * * * * * * * ** * *

"The ego is only an illusion, but a very influential one. Letting the ego-illusion become your identity can prevent you from knowing your true self. Ego, the false idea of believing that you are what you have or what you do, is a backwards way of assessing and living life."
- Wayne Dyer

* * ** * * * * * * * * ** * * * * * * * * * * * * ** * *

"I work really hard at trying to see the big picture and not getting stuck in the ego. I believe we are all put on this planet for purpose, and we all have a different purpose. When you connect with that love and that compassion, that's when everything unfolds."

- Ellen DeGeneres

Fear

Fear can equally become a challenge in opening up your psychic abilities. Fear of the unknown and the worry of bringing in negative energies can affect your development. You must trust and know you are in control and not allow fear to take over. Fear is crippling. You will not be able to progress and fully open your psychic awareness if you are in a constant state of fear. As long as you are working with positive intention (as discussed earlier), you are working with the Light and will attract the same. Faith and trust in a Higher Source and/or Beings is important, regardless of what your belief system is. Ask for God, Angels, your guides, loved ones or any higher energies you believe in, to surround you with their love and protection. I do this every day and know with certainty that they are by my side. You must trust and have complete faith that you are protected.

Are you afraid of receiving a negative message? To easily resolve this fear say an affirmation that you will only receive positive messages. As a psychic I ask not to receive messages of a person's impending death and in turn I do not receive that information.

TIP: Fear will cause you to feel as if you do not have control. Be sure you have control of your psychic gifts and that they are never in control of you. When you are in control, you will not have fear.

"Nothing in life is to be feared, it is only to be understood. Now is the time to understand more, so that we may fear less." - Marie Curie

✳ ✳ ✳✳ ✳ ✳ ✳ ✳ ✳ ✳ ✳ ✳ ✳ ✳ ✳✳ ✳ ✳ ✳ ✳ ✳ ✳ ✳✳ ✳ ✳ ✳ ✳ ✳ ✳ ✳ ✳ ✳ ✳✳ ✳ ✳

"Courage is resistance to fear, mastery of fear, not absence of fear."
- Mark Twain

✳ ✳ ✳✳ ✳ ✳ ✳ ✳ ✳ ✳ ✳ ✳ ✳ ✳ ✳✳ ✳ ✳ ✳ ✳ ✳ ✳ ✳ ✳ ✳ ✳ ✳ ✳ ✳ ✳ ✳ ✳ ✳ ✳✳ ✳ ✳

"I learned that courage was not the absence of fear, but the triumph over it. The brave man is not he who does not feel afraid, but he who conquers that fear."
- Nelson Mandela

✳ ✳ ✳✳ ✳ ✳ ✳ ✳ ✳ ✳ ✳ ✳ ✳✳ ✳ ✳ ✳ ✳ ✳ ✳ ✳ ✳ ✳ ✳ ✳ ✳ ✳ ✳ ✳ ✳ ✳ ✳✳ ✳ ✳

"Only when we are no longer afraid do we begin to live."
- Dorothy Thompson

Outside Influences

Outside influences can particularly impede the process of psychic development. The opinions of others, religious beliefs or disbeliefs, and for some of you, previously learned psychic development concepts that may not resonate with you. Be your authentic self and embrace the gifts of your sixth sense. Do not let another person's viewpoint of psychics or the metaphysical affect you. More importantly, do not let their opinion of whether or not they believe you truly have genuine abilities determine your path of development.

I myself faced this experience. For many years I did not embrace my abilities to the fullest extent because I was afraid of what the response would be from others. As a young adult, a few friends and I were on our way home from the movies when I had a vision of a deer jumping out in front of the car. I saw the deer lying in the road and the dented front bumper of the car. I told the person driving to be careful because a deer might run out in front of the car and a few seconds later we hit a deer. One person in the car said I jinxed it to happen. After that, I kept my visions to myself for years. Many of my family and friends knew that I was interested in psychics and the paranormal, but there were only a few who knew any more than that. When I made the choice to fully embrace my abilities and use them to help others, not everyone in my circle was supportive. Some did not believe I had abilities, others wanted nothing to do with the metaphysical and paranormal and a few just thought I was out of my mind. Through the sadness of the loss of friendships, I still stayed true to myself. I honored the place I was in and I honored the place they were in. They did not need to believe in me. Only I needed to believe in me. All is as it was meant to be. I love what I do and I have an abundance of likeminded friends who are like family to me. Follow your intuition. Listen to your inner voice. Be your authentic self.

"The ultimate ignorance is the rejection of something you know nothing about yet refuse to investigate."
- Dr. Wayne Dyer

* *** * * * * * * * ** * * * * * * * * * * * * * * * * ** * *

"Your time is limited, so don't waste it living some-one else's life. Don't be trapped by dogma – which is living with the results of other people's thinking. Don't let the noise of other's opinions drown out your own inner voice. And most important, have the courage to follow your heart and intuition."
- Steve Jobs

✳ ✳ ✳ ✳ ✳ ✳ ✳ ✳ ✳ ✳ ✳ ✳ ✳✳ ✳ ✳ ✳ ✳ ✳✳ ✳ ✳ ✳ ✳ ✳ ✳ ✳ ✳ ✳ ✳✳ ✳ ✳

"What other people think of you is not your busi-ness. If you start to make that business your business, you will be offended for the rest of your life."
- Deepak Chopra

Religious Beliefs

For some people, throughout the process of psychic development, religious beliefs can become a block-age. If your religious background is the basis of your fear that psychic abilities are taboo or negative, this apprehension will cause you to have a block when receiving messages. Do not allow this fear to control you. It will stagnate your psychic development. If you truly wish to develop your psychic skills you need to commit to yourself and release any past views and worry of religious judgement. Be true to yourself. Remember, we are born with a natural intuition and a sixth sense. If you are reading this book you have already listened to your inner voice.

"Many times we are our worst enemy. If we could learn to conquer our souls, then we will have a much easier time overcoming the obstacles that are in front of us."
- Stephan Labossiere

* * ** * * * * * * * * * * ** * * * * * * * * * * * * * * * * ** * *
"All great changes are preceded by chaos."
- Deepak Chopra

* * ** * * * * * * * * * ** * * * * * * * * * * * * * * * * ** * *
"To be yourself in a world that is constantly trying

to make you something else is the greatest accom-
plishment."
- Ralph Waldo Emerson

The following is a helpful exercise to raise your psychic awareness:

Sit down in a room.

Take three deep breaths.

Look around you.

Become aware of something you see

        AND

Become aware of what you feel

        AND

Become aware of what you hear

        AND

Become aware of your thoughts

All at the same time.

Write down the information you received visually and audibly, along with what you are feeling and thinking. Were you busy looking at everything in the room trying to find the right thing to look at? Did your thoughts jump from one thing to another? Did you lose your focus because you were distracted by the background noise? Did you become preoccupied with how much the toe you stubbed earlier was hurting? This exercise will help you raise your awareness through the realization of the place your mind and ego are at. As you practice and increase your awareness, this exercise will become easier for you.

5

Psychic Protection and Cleansing Your Energy Field

It is extremely important to implement psychic protection while developing your psychic abilities. Negative energies can damage our energy field, which is also known as our aura. Without protection your energy field is vulnerable to all forms of negativity or spirit attachments.

Protecting our personal energy is key to all over well-being, but it is particularly essential when using psychic abilities. Be sure to use psychic protection each time you are working on your psychic abilities. Psychic protection is useful for blocking out all intrusive or negative vibrations from a myriad of sources. In our every day lives we are exposed to various degrees of negativity within our personal relationship, family, friendships, workplace and other establishments. Being aware of protecting your energy field will help to deflect these unhealthy energies, which in turn will keep you in a balanced state. While developing psychically your aura is open to various psychic and spirit energies. Psychic and spiritual protection ensures your energy field is not drained or compromised by these energies.

Keeping a positive and cleansed energy about you enhances not only your psychic awareness but also the livelihood and happiness of your life. Maintaining a positive energy is important to your success and well being over all.

"Your energy introduces you before you even speak." - Unknown

✳ ✳ ✳✳ ✳ ✳ ✳ ✳ ✳ ✳ ✳ ✳ ✳ ✳✳ ✳ ✳ ✳ ✳ ✳ ✳ ✳ ✳ ✳ ✳ ✳ ✳ ✳ ✳ ✳✳ ✳ ✳

"You are the creator of your own experience. You live in a vibrational universe. You have control of the signal that you emit."
- Abraham

✳ ✳ ✳✳ ✳ ✳ ✳ ✳ ✳ ✳ ✳ ✳ ✳ ✳✳ ✳ ✳ ✳ ✳ ✳ ✳ ✳ ✳ ✳ ✳ ✳ ✳ ✳ ✳ ✳✳ ✳ ✳

"Psychic protection isn't about fear. It's like putting your seat belt on or carrying an umbrella."
- Ethan Lazzerini

How To Protect and Cleanse Your Energy Field

Sage/Smudging

Smudging is a Native American cleansing technique to neutralize and remove negative energies. The ritual of smudging involves the burning of sacred herbs in a bowl while reciting a blessing during the cleansing/clearing of an environment or person. Smudging neutralizes and removes negative energies. Sage, sweet grass and incense such as frankincense, sandalwood, sage and myrrh may be used for smudging. Sage is believed to be the most effective in removing negative and toxic energies. White sage is the most common type of sage used for smudging, however there are other forms of sage that can be used. To smudge, light the sage (in a bowl or abalone shell is best) and let it burn a few seconds before blowing out the flame. Gently blow into the sage to produce a smoke. As the smoke rises say a protection prayer. The belief is, as the smoke rises it pulls away any negative energies. Use a feather to fan the smoke if desired. To smudge effectively, work your way around the room with continuity. It is best to finish the cleansing process at the same point from which you start. Be sure to smudge all rooms and corners, as well as doorways, windows and mirrors. If desired, you may include the symbol of the cross over doorways, windows and mirrors. Smudge yourself as well by circling the smoke around you from head to toe while saying a protection prayer.

"Bubble Up"

Protect your energy field and personal space by "bubbling up." When our energy is not protected, it is often affected by negative people and environments. Using the bubble technique is a simple way to ensure protection of your aura. Close your eyes and visualize a ball of white light surrounding and encompassing your entire body. Then envision an invisible bubble all around you, while repeating the words "Only the positive is allowed in, the negative will bounce (deflect) off." By doing this you are consciously blocking your aura from unwanted negative energy. I do this every day, sometimes a few times a day if I am around an increased number of negative people or situations.

Crystals

Crystals contain and emit a powerful energy. Each crystal carries certain properties that aid in healing, love, luck, health, prosperity, manifesting, focusing, and so much more. There are particular crystals that are beneficial for protection and transmuting negative energy. I carry protective and healing crystals with me at all times. I also have them in my home, workplace and car.

The following are a few crystals I like to use for the purpose of protection, cleansing and balancing of energy:

- **Black Tourmaline, Obsidian** and **Smokey Quartz** are great for transmuting and clearing energy.

- **Citrine** is an energizing crystal. It helps to dissipate and transmute negative energies.

- **Clear Quartz** is one of the best stones for cleansing, protection and strengthening the aura. It also amplifies the properties of any other stones it is near, so keeping a piece of quartz around your other stones will increase their effectiveness.

- **Amethyst** cleanses and heals the aura and promotes calm, balance and peacefulness.

- **Hematite** helps to keep the energy field grounded and balanced.

- **Rose Quartz** replaces the aura with love and positivity energy instead of negativity.

- **Labradorite** aids in protecting against psychic attacks or energy "vampires" (those who may draw energy from you knowingly or unknowingly).

Meditation

Meditation, meditation, meditation! As discussed in previous chapters, meditation does a world of good all around. It especially provides protection for our aura by helping release negativity and aiding in grounding and centering. This in turn promotes balance and peacefulness.

Nature

Spending time outdoors, going for a walk, gardening, being near water, and the like are all ways to promote healing and cleansing of your energy field. Additionally, it is also great to bring the outdoors indoor. Add a small water fountain, plants and crystals in rooms or areas you most frequent in your home or workplace. In my reading/ healing room at work I have a small Zen fountain, bamboo plants, a table full of crystals and stones, along with my favorite scented oils and candles. The environment in my room is especially protective, cleansing and healing. I have these items placed throughout my home as well.

Tip: A simple and effective grounding technique is to go outside and hug a tree. Trees, being deeply rooted and connected to the Earth's energy, are grounded and possess a balancing energy.

"An early morning walk is a blessing for the whole day." - Henry David Thoreau

* * ** * * * * * * * * * * ** * * * * * * * * * * * * * * * * * ** * *

"I go to nature to be soothed and healed, and to have my senses put in order."
- John Burroughs

* * ** * * * * * * * * * * ** * * * * * * * * * * * * * * * * * ** * *

"Nature is the great healer, it gives all of itself and only asks to be respected in return. We share a marriage called existence. Crashing waves calm the mind, deep forests soothe the soul. When we touch the Earth it can absorb our woes. All should touch running water, let the wind blow through their hair and gaze at the night sky, for we are all one."
- Virgil Colligan

Water

Taking a shower or going near a body of water is especially cleansing for your energy. Many people are drawn to water without even realizing it is their natural instinct to want to be near what makes them feel good. I love to be by water, especially the ocean. It is so cleansing and revitalizing for the soul. Often, people feel refreshed simply by taking a shower. If you would like to boost cleansing your energy while taking a shower add Epsom salts. As you shower visualize your cares and worries washing away down into the drain. Fill yourself up with white light and the colors of the chakras. If you would like, add relaxing music while practicing this exercise to enhance the cleansing process.

"Being close to the water brings me closer to my soul."
- Steven Aitchison

Protection Prayers

When working on psychic abilities, protect your energy with a protection prayer. I use a simple, but effective, white light protection prayer, which I have included below along with a few others. The White Light Protection Prayer is the prayer I teach students in my development class. You can choose to recite it as your daily protection prayer or you may use a prayer of your preference.

White Light Protection Prayer

I surround myself with the white light of truth. Nothing but that which is of the truth and for my good shall approach me. For I am a child of God and God will protect me.

Angels and Guides Protection Prayer

Archangel Michael, and my angels and guides I invite you in to protect my energy on all levels, for the highest and greatest good. And so it is.

Saint Michael Prayer

(strong protection prayer when working with unknown spirits)

Saint Michael, The Archangel,

Defend us in battle,

Be our protection against the wickedness and snares

of the Devil,

May God rebuke him,

We humbly pray;

and do thou, O Prince of the Heavenly Host,

By the power of God,

Thrust into Hell,

Satan and all evil spirits,

Who wander through the world,

For the ruin of souls.

Amen.

"What lies behind us and what lies before us are tiny matters compared to what lies within us."

- Henry S. Haskins

6

Reading Energy Through Psychometry

Psychometry is the ability to pick up psychic imprints on an object or picture by reading its energy. Psychometry is the "warm up" exercise practiced at the beginning of each psychic development class I teach. Psychometry is of great benefit in developing all of your psychic abilities including "The Clairs" (we will talk more about them in the next chapter) and mediumship.

All objects have an energy imprint that has been left on them from the people that have come in contact with them or from the places the objects have been. Each of us is made of energy and we leave our energetic imprints on all we come in contact with. Reading energy can provide an array of psychic insights and information. The energy vibrations of objects or pictures can offer information on personalities, emotions, physical issues, psychological states, locations and environments. You are reading these vibrations when performing psychometry. For example, ask someone to give you an item or picture of which you do not know the history. If it is an item, hold it in your hands and close your eyes. Do you see any images? What do you feel? Do you feel sad? Happy? Does your arm hurt? What do you hear? Do you sense a female or male energy with the item? Note any impressions and all that comes into your mind while focusing on the item. If it is a picture, look at the picture. What does it say to you? See beyond the surface of what is actually in the picture. How does the picture make you feel? Do you hear or smell anything? If there is a person in the picture does it feel as if they are alive or passed? Sometimes information is received prior to holding an item or after putting the item back down.

Write down any information you receive, whatever enters your mind, whether it makes sense or not, whether it is one word or two pages of words. Do not think—just write. Even if you think the information is jibber jabber. There are sure to be words of wisdom in between it all. Following this guidance will be beneficial for all psychic abilities you are working on developing.

"I have come to accept the feeling of not knowing where I am going. And I have trained myself to love it. Because it is only when we are suspended in mid-air with no landing in sight, that we force our wings to unravel and alas begin our flight. And as we fly, we still may not know where we are

going. But the miracle is in the unfolding of the wings. You may not know where you're going, but you know that so long as you spread your wings, the winds will carry you."

- C. JoyBell C.

7

"The Clairs"

The Clair Senses are psychic abilities that are associated with our physical senses. You may have certain Clair Senses that are more dominant than others.

Clairvoyance

Clairvoyance aka "clear seeing" is the ability to perceive visual information on the past, present and future. These visions could come through at any time during the day as well as through your dreams while you are sleeping. Have you ever had a vision of something happening and then it actually takes place? Do you have dreams that really do come true? A clairvoyant may see visions in their mind's eye or with their physical eyes. Visions may come through as images, symbols or seeing written words. As with many of the other psychic abilities, one of the challenging issues with clairvoyance is the interpretation process of the information being received. Clairvoyance is not as common an ability as other abilities that have been discussed in this book thus far. Visualization techniques, including guided meditations, will help to strengthen natural clairvoyant abilities. Visualization also helps us with understanding spiritual imagery. You may receive images that represent something in particular for you. For instance, you ask for guidance on love and you see the image of the Sun. The sun could represent a time frame being summer or it could represent, feeling happy, bright beginning and so on. Each time you see a specific symbol write it down. In time you will know what each symbol means for you, which in turn will make your interpretation easier.

Affirmation: I am clairvoyant. My clairvoyance is clear. I see visions and psychic messages clearly.

"Seeing occurs, of course, through stopping thought. Thought is the fog. When thought stops in meditation, at any point, we see the other shore."
- Frederick Lenz

Clairsentience

Clairsentience aka "clear feeling" is the ability to sense and retrieve psychic information through feelings and emotions. Many people are clairsentient and are not even aware of it. When you are clairsentient you are able to feel subtle energy and energetic vibrations. Clairsentients have a heightened empathic ability. An empath is someone who has the ability to feel another person's emotions as his or her own. Have you ever been around someone who was in a bad mood and suddenly you realized you were beginning to feel grumpy yourself? An empath absorbs the energy around them like a sponge. If you feel you are an empath be sure to apply the "Bubble Technique" discussed in chapter five. Most people do not realize they have natural clairsentient abilities. Trust your "gut" feelings. Those feelings will always lead you in the right direction. If you have an uneasy feeling about someone or a certain situation then listen to that feeling. Likewise, if you are feeling drawn to someone or feeling good about something, follow through with it. For instance, suppose you have a choice between two jobs. One job offers a lower salary, however when you think of that particular job you feel elated and happy. The other job has a higher paying salary, but there is something you just cannot put your finger on that makes you feel uneasy about it. Follow your initial positive feelings about the first job, rather than the monetary value you would receive by taking the second job. The second job did not make you "feel" good when you focused on it. Trust those feelings, as it is your inner voice guiding you in the direction to make the right choice that is best for you.

Psychometry is a helpful practice exercise to develop clairsentience. Reading the energy of photographs is particularly beneficial. Each time you work on clairsentience sit quietly, just be, and let your physical body become the psychic tool. Close your eyes and just feel. Note anything you are sensing both physically and emotionally.

Affirmation: *I am clairsentient. My clairsentience is clear. I feel energy clearly.*

"Trust the vibes you get, energy doesn't lie."
- Genereux Philip

✳ ✳ ✳✳ ✳ ✳ ✳✳ ✳ ✳ ✳ ✳ ✳✳ ✳ ✳ ✳ ✳ ✳✳ ✳ ✳✳ ✳ ✳ ✳✳ ✳✳ ✳

"I don't look at people the way that some do. I don't look at a person and think they look good, or unattractive, or different. I feel their heart and feel their

soul. I look at their eyes and feel what they are
about. I feel their energy and understand more. You
will miss out on wonderful things if you judge peo-
ple on appearance alone."
- Njari

Clairaudience

Clairaudience aka "clear hearing" is the ability to hear messages from your Higher Self and Spirit both internally in your mind or externally with your ears. Mediums are clairaudiant. These audible messages come through in the form of words or sounds. While working on your clairaudient abilities you may experience pressure or ringing in your ears. The messages received are short and brief, not long winded paragraphs. The key to receiving and interpreting clairaudient messages is to make sure you are writing them down exactly as they are relayed to you. Do not put your own "spin" on the message. For example you may hear the words "car" and "water". If you are keeping a journal you may be compelled to write down, "I need to be careful not to drive my car through a deep puddle during the rainstorm this weekend" or "I have to throw out the water bottle that I left in my car. There must be something wrong with it." In actuality the reason you may have received the words "car" and "water" is because you were simply being given a heads up that you would be going on an impromptu one-day car trip to the beach. As with all of your abilities, you must be aware of overthinking the interpretation. Before you impulsively interpret, wait and see if you receive a little more information. The guidance I offer to my students is to first journal the messages they receive for a few days and then look back through their journal to interpret the meaning. If, after a few days, you are still uncertain of the guidance received, continue journaling until you are able to interpret and understand the message. If you are working on a few abilities at the same time, you may want to combine all of your messages together. Experiment and see what works best for you. A helpful tip is to not allow fear to creep in when using your clairaudient ability. Some people can become unnerved if they audibly hear a spirit with their own ears. Always implement psychic protection when working with spirit energies.

A popular exercise many psychics use to work on clairaudience is to visualize a radio and imagine yourself turning the tuning dial until you are able to hear your messages. Just like a radio you may hear static before receiving a clear sound or sage. Keep practicing and do not give up if you are unable to hear any messages at first.

* * ** * * * *

Affirmation: I am clairaudient. My clairaudience is clear. I hear psychic and spirit messages clearly.

* * ** * * * *

Tip: If you have a difficult time developing your clairaudient ability because of outside distractions, put cotton balls in your ears to block outside noise.

This is especially helpful with your internal hearing.

"The quieter you become, the more you can hear."
- Ram Dass

Claircognizance

Claircognizance aka "clear knowing" is the ability to "know" things without any proof, reason or knowledge. Claircognizants receive information in their mind providing them with an intense sense of "knowing". Claircognizance is the intuitive ability that is being used when we are sure we "know" something although we cannot explain why. For example, your friend tells you she has met a new guy and she thinks he is "the one". You have not met him yourself, but you are being "told" in your mind that he is definitely not "the one" for her. After one date your friend has changed her mind and informs you that they were not compatible. You sensed ahead of time that the relationship was not meant to be. That is claircognizance. Claircognizants are very insightful and they have a strong inner knowing and certainty about things. You may have a difficult time distinguishing between whether the thoughts that pop into your head are your conscious thoughts or whether it is your claircognizance. As mentioned earlier in this book, if you are overthinking then it is your thoughts. A claircognizant thought will come with an instant sense of knowing. Your claircognizance will increase with higher awareness. Meditation, journaling and a healthy diet can help strengthen your claircognizant abilities. Diet is important as healthy nutrients strengthen your cognitive mental function.

* * ** * ** * *

Affirmation: I am claircognizant.
My claircognizance is clear. I am knowing.

* * ** * ** * *

TIP: Trust is essential in developing claircognizance.

Sit down in a quiet place. Now write down whatever pops into your head. You may receive a message from your Higher Self, guides or a passed loved one. This exercise will help you become aware of whether or not you second-guess the information you are receiving. It will help to condition your mind to just trust and "know".

"Claircognizance is the ability to know without trying."

- Lada Ray

8

Working With Auras

Working with auras is a book in itself; however, I have included a brief chapter on auras in this easy guide to psychic development. A general understanding of auras will improve your ability to tune into energy and receive psychic information. As an energy healer I work with auras on a daily basis.

Your aura is also known as your energy field. It is your spiritual signature. The aura is made up of seven layers and each layer relates to our mental, emotional, physical and spiritual health. Sensing and viewing auras is an ability that enables you to receive information about a person's health, feelings, thoughts, emotions, past, present and future. Developing your clairsentient ability will assist in your interpretation of auras.

The colors and size of our aura change as our state of consciousness changes. Our state of consciousness is affected by our life experiences. Do you ever get up in the morning and feel like wearing a particular color? Your state of consciousness often determines what you are drawn to. The color you feel like wearing may be reflecting your state of mind or what you need to wear to enhance your overall well-being.

The main colors associated with auras are similar to that of the chakras, however there are many variations of colors when an aura is viewed. It takes a great deal of practice to interpret the many different color shades. Meanings will be different for shade variations including color shades that are murky and dark. In this chapter we will cover just a few of the positive meanings of the primary shades of the aura.

Aura Colors and Meanings:

Red - Powerful, passionate, energetic, strength

Orange - Adventurous, courage, outgoing, generous

Yellow - Creative, optimistic, playful, intelligent

Green - Social, loving, balance, growth

Blue - Loving, loyal, caring, communicator

Indigo - Artistic, intuitive, sensitive, visionary

Violet/Purple - Mystical, intuitive, visionary, wisdom

White -Spiritual, purity, higher dimensions, transcendent (when white is a primary color in the aura, not the initial color seen before other colors)

Gold - Enlightenment, wisdom, connectedness with higher beings

The following are a few simple exercises to learn how to sense and view auras:

Sensing Auras

Exercise 1:

Use this as a "warm up" exercise to tune into energy:

1. Rub your palms together for a few seconds.

2. Face your palms toward each other

3. Bring your palms as close together as possible without them physically touching.

4. Now move them slightly away from each other.

5. Move them towards each other again.

6. Feel the energy between your pals as you are doing this.

Exercise 2:

Practice this exercise on a person or a pet:

1. Close your eyes.

2. Hold your palms just a few inches above an area of your subject's body.

3. Move your palms closer to their body until you

feel a change in the energy. This is their aura.

The energy will feel as it did between your palms in the previous exercise.

It may be closer to their physical body or it may be farther away, depending on whether they are personally feeling open or closed off. Someone who is more guarded will have an energy field close to their body. The energy ball exercise discussed in chapter seven under the sub-topic of clairsentience, is beneficial to use when learning to work with auras.

Viewing Auras

Exercise 1: *Viewing Your Own Aura*

1. Stand in front of a mirror. Lighting should be soft and not casting shadows.

2. Stare just over your shoulder or the top of your head.

3. Let your eyes go slightly out of focus.

4. Write down what you see and experience.

Exercise 2:

1. Look at a picture on the wall.

2. Fixate your eyes on a particular spot on the picture.

3. Let your eyes go slightly out of focus.

4. Using your peripheral vision, while still staring at the spot, notice if there is a hazy outline around the picture. Most often you will see a white outline first and then begin to see colors of the aura.

You can apply these same exercises when viewing a specific person. Some people have a natural ability to work with energy and auras. Others may not be comfortable working in another person's energy. You will know which abilities resonate most with you. Trust your intuition.

Tip: Tuning into and understanding your own aura will accelerate your development of interpreting auric information for yourself and others.

"The aura given out by a person or object is as much a part of them as their flesh."

- Lucian Freud

9

Telepathy and Remote Viewing

Telepathy

Telepathy aka "distance feeling" is the ability to communicate thoughts from one mind to another without using any of the physical senses. Have you ever been thinking of someone and then that person calls you out of the blue? Was there a time you looked at a friend and you both knew what each other was thinking without speaking? Telepaths have the ability to mentally send and receive information. Some telepaths are better at sending than receiving or vice versa. As your awareness opens you will become more in tune with your telepathic ability. Students in my psychic development class have a lot of fun practicing telepathy. I will share with you some easy exercises that will help you with developing telepathy. As in Kreskin's Board Game, using colors, symbols and numbers is a basic way to work on your telepathic skills. For instance, take a few color cards, mix them up, and then choose the color you feel is on each card before you turn it over. Another basic exercise is to place pieces of colored paper under cups, close your eyes, switch the cups around and then guess which color is under each cup. If you are practicing with another person, one of you thinks of a color and sends that color to the other person. See if the person receives the color that was sent. Start out with basic primary colors first. Another simple exercise is to think of a person you would like to hear from and see if that person shortly thereafter communicates with you. I had a student who one day was practicing telepathy by sending a telepathic message to her husband to bring her home a sandwich. A few hours later he walked in the door with a sandwich for her. He told her that he suddenly had the thought she might like a sandwich. Her husband was stunned when she told him she had been sending him that message telepathically all day. As with other psychic abilities, before practicing telepathy clear your head through meditation, nature or whatever method works for you.

TIP: Visualize a white stream of light flowing from your forehead to the other person's forehead. Picture whatever you are sending moving through that stream of light from you to the other person.

"*First begin between selves, set a definite time, at each at that time put down what the other is doing. Do this for 20 days. You shall find you have the key to telepathy.*"
- Edgar Cayce

* *** * * * * * * * * ** * * * * * * * * ** * * * * * * * ** * *

"Do you believe in telepathy? No? Then what are you doing when you pray?"
- Charles R. Moore

* * ** * * * * * * * ** * * * * * * * * * * * * * * * * ** * *

"There is a voice that doesn't use words. Listen."
- Rumi

Remote Viewing

Remote viewing is the ability to perceive and describe a person, object, place or event that is distant or concealed. It is also known as our "second sight". A remote viewer is able to recognize information that is not obvious to their physical senses, regardless of time or space. An example of remote viewing is misplacing an item and receiving an impression that it is under the sofa in the living room. Remote viewing is a mental ability that can help expand your mind and strengthen your trust in your intuitive abilities.

How to Remote View

Meditation is essential to accurate remote viewing. Meditation will help you achieve intense focus and concentration, which is necessary to view remotely.

Steps to follow:

- Close your eyes so you are not visually distracted.
- Meditate to clear your mind.
- Focus and concentrate on what you want to remote view.
- Be open to receiving information, impressions and images.
- Write down what you receive.

In psychic development class we practice a remote viewing exercise I call "The Box". Before class begins I put a variety of items in a box and the class has to describe what items they perceive are in the box. I have them write down any information they receive, including colors, shapes, patterns, item descriptions and so on. I also incorporate telepathy into this exercise. As the class is doing the exercise, I think of the items that I put into the box. Students have the choice to write down what they obtained through remote viewing and/or what they received telepathically from me. This is a fun exercise that can be used to develop one or more than one psychic ability at the same time.

An alternate exercise is to remote view a particular location. Have someone give you an address they know details about, but that you have no knowledge of. Describe what you remote view at that address— the type of house, surroundings, landscape —any information you receive. Then have the person who gave you the address validate your information.

Tip: Do not overthink and let your thoughts crowd out the information you are given. If you are practicing exercises like the ones above, write down your initial impressions, no matter what it is you receive.

"Remote viewing is a discipline that can heighten the awareness of our strong senses and intuitions and can be used for personal growth and spiritual development. Because remote viewing can be used in either way, it's potential for growth, healing, and exploration is tremendous."

- JZ Knight

10

Astral Travel

Astral travel aka astral projection is the conscious ability to leave your body. It is also known as an out-of-body experience (OBE). Astral travel can be achieved through meditation, lucid dreaming, or while awake. During astral projection the astral body leaves the physical body and travels into the non-physical or spirit world (astral plane). The astral body is the spiritual equivalent of the physical body. Everyone is capable of astral traveling, however some people have the natural ability of astral projection, while others have to work harder to develop it. Many people astral project and just do not remember doing it. Oftentimes, this occurs while sleeping when the physical mind is asleep and the subconscious mind is able to take over. When you are out of body you are free to go wherever you want to go and there is no time or distance.

Astral travel was my older sister Jeanie's favorite ability. One of my fondest recollections of this ability is the first time my sister shared her gift of astral travel with me. She told me she had "visited" me the night before through astral projection. My sister, who was nine years older than I, was already married and living in a different town. She described the pajamas I had worn, the purple bear I had on my bed and the TV show I had on. My initial response was to tell her to stop spying on me because it was creepy. Then I asked her how she does it. From then on astral travel became second nature to me, as it can for you too.

There are many benefits to learning how to astral

project. You can:

- Visit any place in the Universe-people, towns, states, countries, planets.
- Visit passed loved ones.
- Meet your guides and angels.
- Activate healing by accessing the subconscious to find the root of the condition. Often sickness is caused by emotional damage.

How to Astral Travel:

Relaxation is necessary to experience astral travel. Your body must be completely relaxed, as if you were asleep, but your mind is still awake. Meditation is the best way to achieve this. If preferred there are guided meditations available specifically for astral travel.

Have the confidence that you *will* astral travel.

Do not let fear get in the way. Do not be afraid of dying or being unable to get back into your physical body. Your physical and astral bodies are attached by a silver cord so there is no need to worry about having difficulty returning.

Maintaining the level of concentration needed to astral travel may be one of your toughest obstacles. Use the techniques discussed earlier in this book to help you resist distractions and stay focused.

The separation process from the physical body may be a startling experience the first time you astral project. Your body may shake or vibrate and you may hear loud noises or cracking sounds. The experience may initially overwhelm you and throw you off balance. Take your time and keep practicing. Work on raising your astral arms and legs first. Then move on to raising your head. The head has the strongest connection to the physical body so it can take longer to detach.

There are various methods you can use to astral travel. One of the most common methods is to roll out of your body as if you were rolling out of bed. Another way is to pull yourself up and out of your body as if you were sitting up from a laying down position. If you would like, you can visualize yourself leaning on an object, like a table, to help you separate from your physical body. Some people are able to astral project through lucid dreaming by consciously being in control of the dream. When you are able to achieve separation from your physical body make sure you move your astral body away from your physical body, so that your astral body is not pulled back into it by the magnetic pull between the two bodies. Once you have moved away from your physical body you can travel to wherever you please. It is best to begin with keeping it simple by moving just above your body, through a window, door, or the roof. Once you become comfortable with astral travel you will only need to think of where you want to go and you will go there. Do not become frustrated if you are not able to astral travel right away. It is an ability that takes much practice.

Tip: If you practice astral projection when you are tired, you will fall asleep. You want to remain in control of your conscious mind when you astral travel.

"Blessed are those that know the path out of their carnal flesh, for they shall attain intuition."
- Michael Bassey Johnson

11

Mediumship and Spirit Communication

Mediumship is the ability to communicate with spirits. All mediums are psychic, but not all psychics are mediums. Everyone has the ability to sense when their loved ones are around, however a medium acts as a channel for spirits and is able to interact with them. A medium must raise his or her vibration and at the same time a spirit must lower their vibration in order to communicate with each other.

When I was young, even though I could see and hear

spirits, I did not communicate with them. I was not able to communicate with the spirit world as I do now because, I did not know how and quite frankly I was so scared I did not want to.

The first step to developing your mediumship abilities is wanting to. You do not have to communicate with the spirit world if you don't want to. If you are uncomfortable seeing or hearing spirits, let the spirits know you would prefer not to communicate with them. You may be comfortable interacting with spirits but perhaps need to set boundaries. For example, if I do not want to be awoken by spirits while I'm sleeping, I set that intention before I fall asleep.

The next step is to be sure your desire to develop mediumship abilities is with the right intent. The intention for spirit communication should be to receive messages to guide and help yourself, others, or the spirits. Once you have the desire and positive intention, it is important to focus on strengthening your psychic ability. By doing so, it will raise your vibration to a high enough level to achieve spirit communication. It is necessary to apply all of the techniques previously discussed in this book that help raise psychic awareness. The more often you meditate, stay grounded and centered, cleanse your energy, and hold good intention, the higher your vibration will be. Additionally, it is of the essence you use a protection prayer when practicing mediumship, as you will have access to all types of energies in the spirit realm.

Spirits communicate through symbols, images, and words. Some mediums, myself included, are also able to interpret the emotions and feelings of spirits through energy. This is a gift I am grateful to have as it helps me connect effectively to spirit. Group environments are especially helpful for working on mediumship skills. I highly recommend practicing with like-minded people or joining a psychic development class. It is a productive way to receive confirmation and validation about the spirits you are communicating with.

How to's:

1. Close your eyes.

2. Take three deep breaths

3. Say your protection prayer and/or call in your guides.

4. Focus on whom you wish to communicate with and set your intention.

5. Sit quietly and listen.

6. Journal – write down your experience and what you receive.

7. Protection prayer and cleanse (i.e. sage).

I work with energy as a psychic and as medium. Each time I connect with a spirit I feel how they passed. I also feel any issues or illnesses, emotionally, mentally or physically, that they may have experienced in their lifetime. Feeling spirit energy in this manner can be challenging whether you are just learning mediumship or more advanced. A tip to help with this type of experience is to not allow that feeling to control you. I receive the initial feeling and once I have that information I immediately "push" it out by saying in my mind, "Thank you, now please release this (feeling, sadness, pain..." Whatever you are experiencing at that moment that you do not want). You want to be in control. ***You never let a spirit control you.***

Some people struggle with multiple spirits coming through all at once. Again, you want to be in control. If you are communicating with a particular spirit and others start to push their way through, remain in control. Tell the other spirits that they have to wait their turn and continue communicating with your initial spirit until you have received their messages. Then, if you choose, you can move on to the other spirits one at a time. Occasionally, a spirit may be too close to your energy field and is drawing too much of your energy. When a spirit is in my energy space, I begin to feel anxious and my heart will race. Tell the spirit to step back just a little so that you can communicate with them. The spirit will listen to you if they want you to be able to receive their message.

The ability to communicate with spirits is gratifying but also a responsibility not to be taken lightly. You are the messenger and learning to interpret spirit messages accurately takes time. Journaling has a central role in helping you with the interpretation of how spirit messages come through specifically for you. Each time you are practicing mediumship apply all techniques discussed in the awareness and blockages chapters of this book.

Tip: *Do not use a Ouija board.* As a paranormal investigator I have experienced many unfortunate situations involving negative energies that were caused by the use of a Ouija board. The boards are used as a portal to other dimensions and can be an opening for dark entities.

"The Spirit World is able to get through to you easily when your mind is still and clear. Meditation is of-

ten referred to as 'sitting in the silence'. Whenever you want to reach Spirit from this side of life, start by sitting in silence."
- James Van Praagh

✶ ✶ ✶✶ ✶ ✶ ✶ ✶ ✶ ✶✶ ✶ ✶ ✶ ✶ ✶ ✶ ✶ ✶ ✶ ✶ ✶ ✶ ✶ ✶ ✶ ✶ ✶ ✶✶ ✶ ✶

"There is the world of the flesh, and there is the Spirit World. When the flesh is gone, the Spirit forever remains. Their voices speak to those who know how to listen. Wisdom is born in the heart, and then spoken."
-Wolf Clan Song

12

Closing Thoughts

There are many different types of psychic abilities. This book covered only a few of the psychic abilities that you may be interested in exploring and developing. For some of us, learning how to tap into our psychic abilities helped us to embrace our authentic self. Maybe you have had a journey similar to mine or would just like to understand and learn about psychic abilities and mediumship. No matter what brought you to reading this book, you were meant to read it. Everything happens for a reason. By embracing my psychic abilities, I have been able to help many people. I have experienced a wealth of personal growth on my psychic journey and have learned much about myself and the Beyond, and so can you. I am grateful for my psychic gifts and could not imagine my life any other way. Developing your psychic abilities may take time, but the journey will be a rewarding one. If practiced regularly, psychic development will change your life.

Love, Light and Happiness to all! :-)

Jacqui Geary

"All is at it should be."
- Frederick Lenz

About Jacqui Geary

Jacqui Geary is a gifted Psychic Medium, Intuitive Tarot Reader, Angel Card Reader and Energy Healing Therapist. She is owner of Trinity Metaphysical Center and founder of East Coast Research and Investigation Paranormal Team (ECRIPT). Jacqui saw her first spirits at a young age and being intrigued with the paranormal throughout childhood, participated in her first ghost hunt over 30 years ago. As a reader, Jacqui is able to provide insight and guidance in all areas of your life—past, present and future—to help you on your life path or to connect you with passed loved ones. She uses her gifts every day to help others and teaches frequent classes and workshops. Jacqui has been featured on radio shows, documentaries, newspapers, magazines and other various media. She is currently co-host of Among

The Realms Radio show to help educate others on the metaphysical and paranormal.

For more information about Jacqui please visit: www.TrinityMetaphysicalCenter.com.

Namaste

"I honor the place in you which is of love, truth, light, and peace."